The Runaway Mommy

The Runaway Mommy

First edition: December 2013
Printed in the USA
The Runaway Mommy / Jane Kuo Paris, Scott Rim.
ISBN: 978-0615927985

www.runaway-mommy.com

This book is dedicated to my sons,
and to my mother and father

JKP

Dedicated to my Mother

SR

Once there was a mommy who wanted to run away. So she said to her bunny, "I am going to run away."

"If you run away," said her bunny, "I will run after you,
for you are my mommy."

"If you run after me," said the mommy, "I will go to New York City and get an apartment in Chelsea, and I'll buy a white couch."

"If you go to New York City," said the bunny, "I'll move in with you and drink my grape juice on the couch."

"Sorry mommy."

"If you follow me to New York," said the mommy, "I will go to Barcelona, where I will take siestas every day and go flamenco dancing at night."

"If you go to Barcelona," said the bunny, "I will follow you and go dancing with you."

"But I won't nap!"

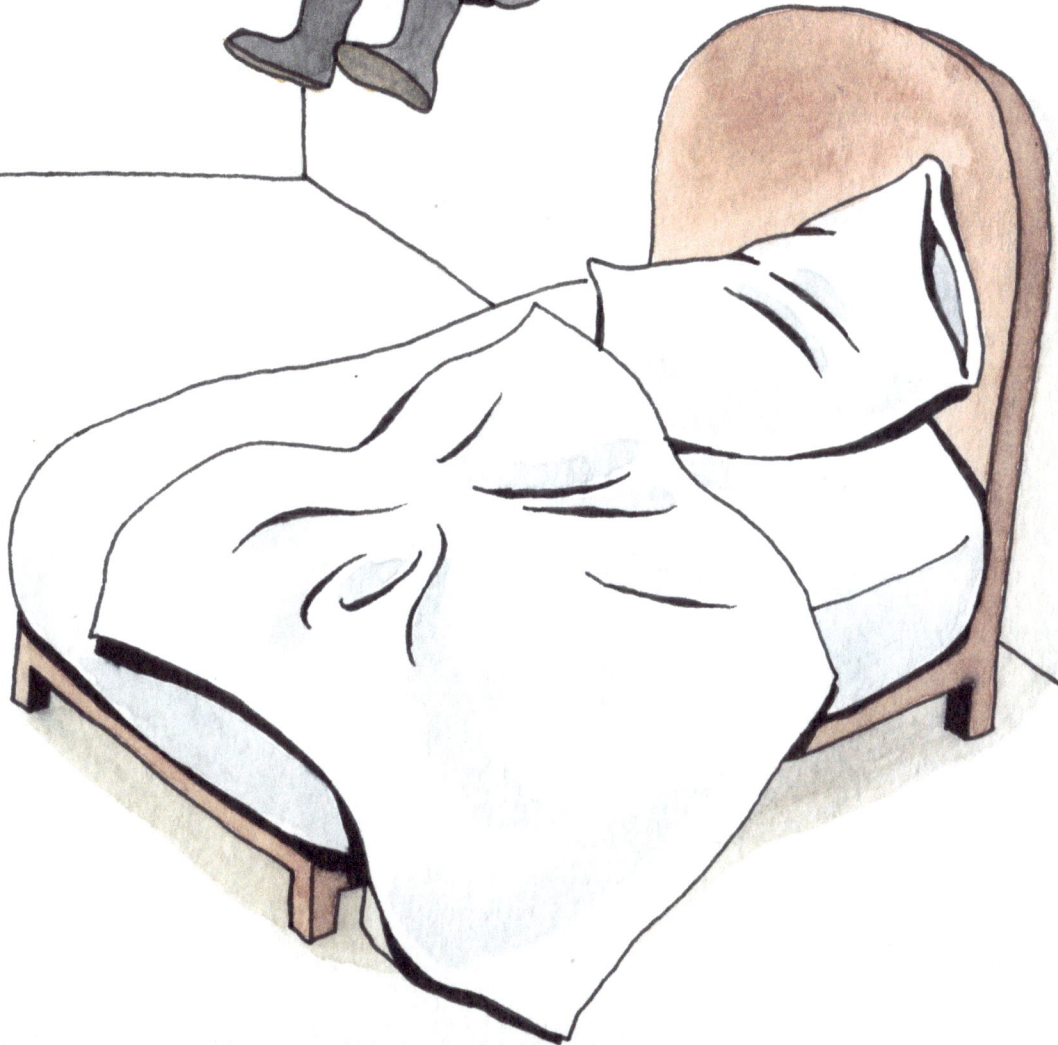

"If you follow me to Barcelona," said the mommy, "I will go to San Francisco and work at a tech startup."

"If you go to San Francisco and work at a tech startup," said the bunny, "I'll hang out at the office and grab energy drinks from the fridge."

"He's wired in."

"If you follow me to San Francisco," said the mommy, "I will go to a battleground state and intern for a presidential candidate."

"If you go to a battleground state," said the bunny, "I will follow you and be the baby that your candidate has to kiss."

"On second thought..."

"If you follow me to a battleground state," said the mommy,

"I will go to medical school and become a trauma surgeon."

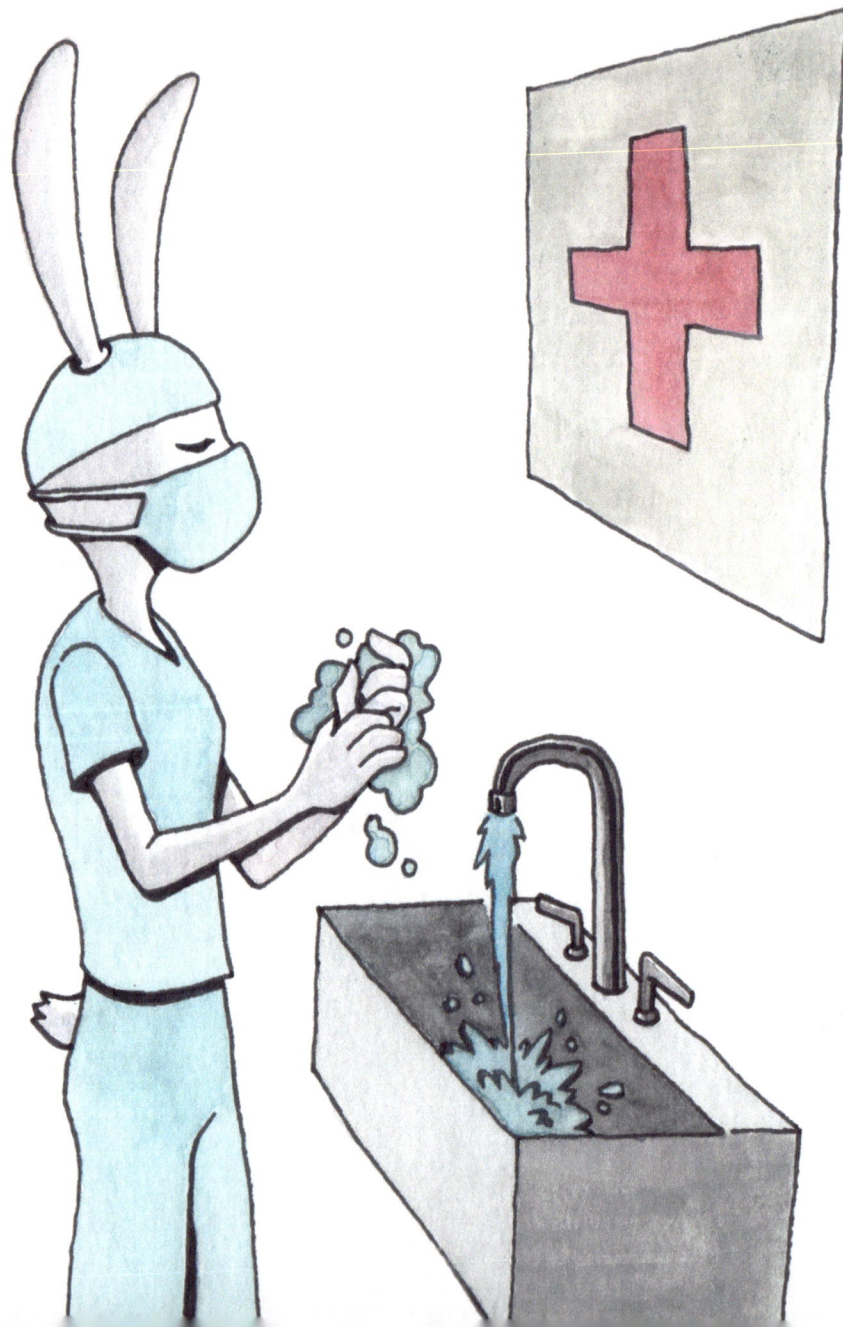

"If you go to medical school and become a surgeon," said the bunny, "I will follow you into the operating room and be your helper."

"Forceps, mommy?"

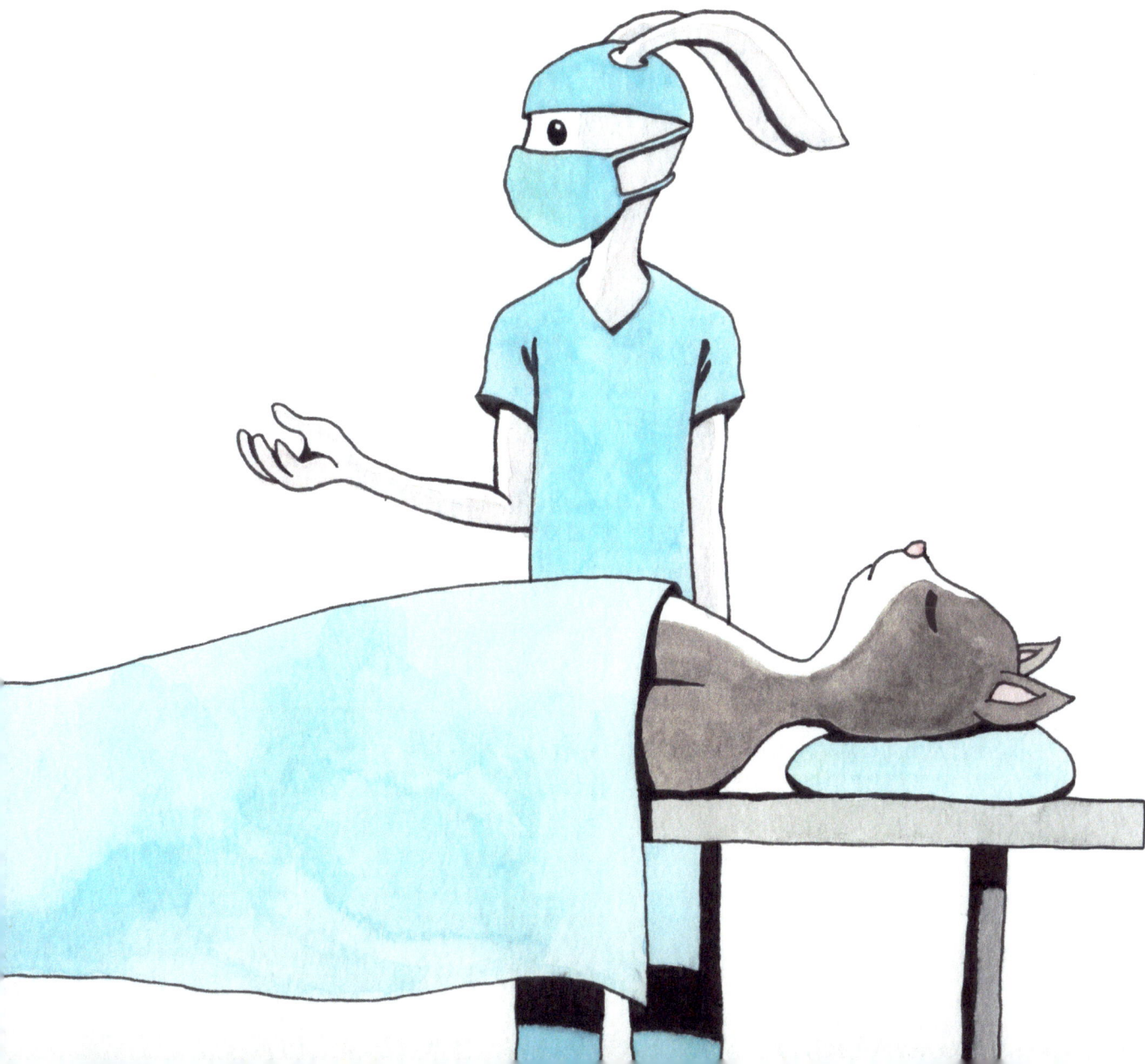

"If you follow me to the operating room," said the mommy, "I will become a consultant and travel the world and earn a million frequent flyer miles."

"If you become a consultant and travel the whole world," said the bunny, "I'll sneak into your luggage and be with you wherever you go, for you are my mommy."

"I like the idea of seeing the world with you," said the mommy.

"So do I," said the bunny.

"Mommy, can I have carrot cake?"

Jane Kuo Paris is a mother to two boys, who are a constant source of wonder and inspiration. She was born in Taiwan, grew up in Los Angeles and now lives in the San Francisco Bay Area with her husband and children.

Scott Rim is an illustrator and visual designer hailing from the Chicago and San Francisco area. He currently lives in Pasadena, California and likes bikes, animation and frisbees.

www.ingramcontent.com/pod-product-compliance
Lightning Source LLC
Chambersburg PA
CBHW042105040426

42448CB00002B/145